MONKEY SCREAMS

<<<

ROBERT JOE STOUT

>>>

FUTURECYCLE PRESS

www.futurecycle.org

Library of Congress Control Number: 2015938025

Published by FutureCycle Press
Lexington, Kentucky, USA

ISBN 978-1-938853-75-3

For Paul, Emily, Ingrid, Deirdre and Noah

CONTENTS

TESTIMONIES FROM VIETNAM

Hero..9

Messenger..10

Good Reports...12

Propaganda Photos...16

In Command...18

God's Grandeur..19

Yankee Know How..20

Purple Heart...21

Signals...22

Supply Clerk...23

Second Lieutenant...24

Ambush..26

Night Patrol..28

Why?..29

Day After Cease-Fire..30

AN ENEMY TO BLAME

Baby Boomer Dentist..35

Telephone Installer...36

Account Clerk...38

Teenagers..40

Junior High Music Teacher..42

English Professor..44

Football Coach...46

County Assessor...48

Registered Nurse...50

Disability Pensioner..52

Welfare Applicant...54

Small Business Owner...56

BELIEVING IN HIS DREAMS

Writer...61

Morning..62

Redoing an Old Humor Piece..63
Words..64
Language..65
Interruption..66
A Simple Meal...67
Friends Appear..68
Best Friend...69
When He Was Just a Tyke...70
Agnostic...71
Santa Cruz Amilpas, Oaxaca..72
Monthly Checkup..73
Obituary: Freedom Fighter...74
Survivor...75
Different...76
Fan 77
Philosopher..78
Gourmet at Seventy-nine...79
A Good Book..80
Alone in Mexico..81
A Million Dancing Lights..82
The Other..83

Acknowledgments

‹‹‹
TESTIMONIES FROM VIETNAM
›››

HERO

Sweat slides down my neck
but I don't move. I try to remember things
so I can tell my dad and mom
just how it was, my dress blues on,
a one-star pacing back and forth
in front of us, the Marine band
—I'll tell them medals, not shots
and screams, sudden bursts
of hand grenades, shattered fragments
of my radio embedded everywhere.
I'll tell them how they called my name,
how I stood straight, responded
with a crisp salute. Not tell them
four Marines with blankets
where their legs had been
sit waiting here for decorations
just like mine. Nor that the major
with a loppy face gets his pinned on
and we all know he got his wound when rocks
—not shrapnel—bruised his legs and shin.
He looks so proud; he likes this show.
Not me. I close my eyes. Hear
trip mines click. Smell Agent Orange.
Sense shadows moving towards me.
Kill some more VC.

MESSENGER

"Hey, sailor, here we are!" I nod, grab
my duffel bag, time the launch's gentle
bumping up against old tires that protect the dock.
"Good luck!" the helmsman calls—*good luck?*
I wave but don't look back. He didn't ask,
I didn't say, just bummed an up-the-river ride
—it happens all the time out here. Some GI
looking for a girl he loved, a buddy's grave,
some buried loot, so he comes back to places
like this sprawl of huts and tents
and blown-up streets—like all the rest,
I tell myself, then look for someone
who can tell me where things are.
"Orphanage?" A tall blond Seabee squints
and blinks. "No, hell...oh, you mean like, yeah,
some nuns—they're gooks..." He twists his fingers
as though trying to grasp a tool
he's never used before. "Yeah, up that road
two clicks, I guess—or maybe three." I toss
my duffel bag across my shoulder
—even in the heat to stretch out, walk,
feels good. I find a little store,
buy some beer, drink and walk and rest
and walk and drink again. And then I'm there.
It's nothing much. Gray cement walls,
thatched roofs. I see a bunch of skinny kids
hopping up a path. I sigh and climb.
A nun beside an open doorway folds
her hands and stares. Her face is small,
her exposed wrists mere bone. "You speak...?"
I start to ask; she shakes her head.
I kneel, untie the duffel bag, extract
a picture and an envelope. The note
inside is short—half a page of scribbles

I can't read; the rubber band around the picture
circles sixty fifty-dollar bills.
She takes my hand in hers—a sparrow's
touch—I feel her tears against my wrist.
"You...so, so berry good," she chokes.
I close my eyes. Hear bombs exploding,
gunboats strafing shore. And whisper, "No,
bad, so bad..." and wish the money
that I bring her could feed more.

GOOD REPORTS

1.

The river flows beneath the jungle's opulence,
the cloud-dotted sky strident blue overhead.
The patrol boat's throbbing comes up through me;
I feel its engines as my own blood and breathing,
just us, alone—alone within a timeless
something I can sense, not grasp, the all-creating
Buddha-universe, jungle, river, sky.
Perched on the edge of it, a stranger, interloper,
uniformed for war, I breathe awareness
of the flowing of myself; the rising
sun brings clarity, brings warmth.
Brings increments of noise, each sound distinct,
each insect vocalist plucking a separate nerve.
One doesn't think—one just absorbs sensations
as they come: the lapping water,
mossy pencels, herons flapping wings,
ramjet engine throbbing a heavy song
beyond the hills. I know this river's kindnesses
and quirks; it and the boat are heart
and blood of a vast unity of which,
a cell, I am a part. I know when creatures
not a part of us intrude. ARVN. NVA.
U.S. Marines on patrol. I know
—and know that my enemies,
like me, have merged into the entity.
What I feel, they feel too: disruption
of the harmony, a change of ripples, rhythms
—fleas upon the Buddha's calm. "Ahead
four knots," I tell the helm. The river parts
and gives us Buddha's smile.

2.

Sliding through a swath of sunlight,
jungle giving way to farms around us,
big-bellied transports dropping towards the runways
to our right. The muddy water
rimmed with rustproof plastic, detritus
of the war behind us, metal roofs
and concrete walls ahead. Our faces shed
their squinting like old netting giving way,
and I sense laughter in the air around me
—seamen talking whores and haircuts, Schlitz
and letters from back home. Lines out,
the gangplank down, I feel lighter, younger;
horns and shouts, air hammers, squealing brakes
bombard ruminations about good meals and women,
how a stiff mixed drink will taste. Civilians
peal away to let me pass—*What is
it like to be out there?* Covert blinking
in their eyes. I swagger just a little,
like I did in high school after football games,
carelessly return the Shore Patrol salutes.
"A day or two," I tell the desk clerk
at the TOQ, get my keys, collect my mail
and, perched on the wooden window sill
to open packages from home,
sense human shouts outside, an oily grit
fouling the air, walls that absorb,
give nothing back. Hands in my lap,
I sit and blink at new gift shoes,
dried fruit, tinned hams and seek
the faces of the ones I love
—but nothing comes. Then green. Jungle birds.
Heart beating to patrol boat's pulse.
I live out there. Here I am less. An actor
in a dream who can't wake up.

3.

Fly-crusted pieces of two mangled buffaloes
twist in a current pushing them
against protruding swamp tree roots.
"We shot 'em, man! Blew 'em apart!"
Glasses sliding down his nose,
a gunner trembles as he tries to grin.
I push between two corpsmen.
Branum squints through morphined haze.
We went straight in!
Bloody froth softens the words.
I start to curse, louder as the Evac copter
rips caps from our heads, roils water
into green-gray smocking. On deck ten feet away
the CO, a JG like me, puffs freckled cheeks
as he exhales. *Straight fuckin' into ambush!*
I air it out. The corpsmen shove the gurney
past my clasp on Branum's hand. "He'll be okay,"
the younger of them whispers. One fist thumbs up
—a futile wave—and I watch the copter rise,
plants thrashing in its airy wake,
and "Right fuckin' into ambush!" blaspheme
the amateurs the Navy sends
into channels where green is a language
one has to learn by speaking ripples,
hearing palm fronds, feeling birds.

4.

BIC sticking to my fingers
where I've squeezed the plastic trying to write,
I jab at the report—but in mind's eye
I see the helos roaring treetop high,
VC firing back, napalm flashing
on the water, sheets of brilliant orange
smoldering into smells of sizzling foliage,
burning flesh. "VC's dispersed..." I force back thought.
"Canal safe for movement now..."
Instead of bright birds chattering
in the shredded growth, I hear Sesny
(soon to be LC) pace the floor a month ago.
"There was no need to take that risk..."
Hear my teeth grind inside my head.
"I knew what I was doing, sir. I sensed..."
"Sensed *hell!* You had orders!"
Orders? Orders to stay safe?
Guess Cong weren't there? Falsify reports?
"Yessir," my mouth so dry the sibilants
stuck against my teeth. As they do now.
He doesn't want to win this war.
He wants his leaf and doesn't care
what lies it takes to get it.
That's what this fucking war's about:
promotion based on good reports.
Forget doped minds and body bags,
arms blown off by booby traps,
the smells of Willy Pete.

PROPAGANDA PHOTOS

Every time the seabird tilts
I see the Gulf of Tonkin spread
a hundred shades of emerald, turquoise,
mauve beyond the surf's white froth.
"Hard to believe there's war down there,"
the most loquacious of the camera guys chitchats.
He's been to Phu Kim once or twice: "A fucking jewel,
little cement houses, man, all neat and painted,
pretty women, a fucking paradise!" We circle twice;
Airborne is landing copters filled with troops.
They glare at our shaved faces and clean uniforms.
"Oh shit!" I hear the camera guy exclaim.
The vacant village has a charred and moldy stench.
"There's no one left..." an airborne gapes.
The pretty little houses are all half blown apart.
A stressed interrogator-type runs up.
"Out! Get those cameras out of here!"
"Fuck you!" I snap. Then, "Do your job
and I'll do mine!" But film clips? "No,"
I tell the crew and hold them back.
In what looks like a hermitage—schoolhouse, perhaps—
a Pfc stands with his feet apart, weapon
dangling from his wrist. "Are you all..." *right?*
I start to ask, then see his face.
Tears and snot stream through his beard,
drip down his chin onto his chest. I touch
a shoulder that's like frozen beef.
"We hung out here—almost four months,"
a corporal scuffing up behind me says.
"He had a girl—a pretty thing, spoke English, too."
I nod, sense more than hear the corporal's words:
"The VC never bothered us but, fuck,
they knew. They do that, man. Hide
and wait and kill the ones who help us out."

I see him put his arm around his buddy's waist.
"Come on, you guys!" My voice a snarl
more than a shout. "We're in the way.
We'll take our pretty pictures somewhere else."

IN COMMAND

Beyond glimmering green
of rice stalks sifting the hot breeze,
the jungle's threats lie coated
with a fine white mist. The rain has lifted
but the air exudes the rotting stench
of vegetation mulching into mud.
Mosquitoes rise in swirling clouds
around the harvestmen and women
moving slowly through flooded paddies
as far as I can see. Two GIs
stand together on the levee, nodding
as they smoke their cigarettes. I check
my watch, decide to give them
five more minutes, then get them moving
back along the field's perimeter.
They hate this duty even though it's safe.
One night two young privates
thought they heard berserkers
and wounded three half-starved kids.
Another night two of them shot
and damned near killed each other.
I sigh and head towards my two soldiers.
They look up and, seeing me,
high sign with crooked fingers, move apart.
I wave and turn but soggy ground
gives way beneath my weight. I grab at sticks
and stalks but keep on sliding,
shout for a hoist but they can't hear me,
finally—flopping, slipping, wading
—get my footing, worm my way
back to the levee,
curse this fucking war.

GOD'S GRANDEUR

These damned paths end. You think you know
just where you are and man you're lost.
Like now. Trees with great big sweating leaves
drape rocks that gleam like jade. I crouch,
work past the leaves, crawl up a slope.
Safe here, they say, miles from the Cong
—you never know. The fucking jungle's
like a song that just goes on and on.
I want to pray but nothing comes so I push on.
Find a place that I can sit. The sunshine
on the shimmering green is like a thousand
sparkling lights. Birds in the trees,
a gentle breeze—*God's grandeur, man!*
The tears start in my guts, dry out
before they hit my eyes. *I hate this place!*
Hate it with an intensity so fucking fierce
I think I going to come apart. *Controls y'se'f...*
That's what my auntie used to say.
She talked her "Heaven" all the time
and pictured this. Birds. Green leaves.
Clear endless sky. I bow my head but still can't pray.
Open my pack. The letter's there. The photographs.
Two comic books. Hurt flings hailstorms
through my chest. *Who am I? Fuck!*
And where? And why? I lift the books,
look at the pictures, try to read
the words. It helps. It's home.
I close my eyes. Tears start to come.
I still can't pray. Cong shaped like Batman,
Robin, Joker dance across my mind.

YANKEE KNOW HOW

"Yankee Know How!" The old fart twists
the jeep around big mixers pouring concrete
for the fill. I nod, then ask how much it costs
to build two miles of road through river
overflow. He yanks his cap tight down
across his brow and laughs. "No problem, son!
Money we've got!" A foreman straddling two-by-fours
waves and shouts, "Martini time!" The old fart
laughs and shows a thumbs-up fist, then jams
the jeep along a road that's mostly mud
and rocks. Strange turtle creatures slide
along a wood line through a slough.
I look again: Vietnamese in their straw hats,
up to their necks in mud. "Fools farming there!"
The old fart honks the horn to chase
two women off the road. Then—"Oh shit!"
—he hits the brakes rounding a turn.
I grab the windshield with both hands;
sky hurtles past, the muddy slough,
the bawling face of a huge buffalo.
It caroms across fenders, hood; I jump,
feel the jeep's tires spin, try to get up,
the beast's huge body rolling over mine,
evade its hooves as it goes bellowing
into the mud. "Hey? You okay? No broken bones?"
The old fart tries to help me up.
His face is cut; his cap is gone;
a reef of slobber glistens on his chin.
"See why we need the fucking roads!"
He waves both fists at the wounded beast,
the Vietnamese, the river oozing blood.

PURPLE HEART

A hundred meters down the street
a crushed can gleams. I stop, weight
forward on the canes they've issued me
to hobble here and there in Tokyo. A thousand things
that I could focus on—the whole world passing
like concentric speeding trains
—and yet I see the can. Shiny things
where I come from bring death.
I start to lift my hand—then spin
My weapon! What the hell…? I grab
a wall to keep from falling,
slowly turn. No one is watching—no one
cares. I blink. There's no barbed wire
anywhere. The cars speed by, their drivers
grinning, chatting, peering straight ahead.
The only thing they have to fear
is getting home too late. I want to shout
to everyone *This isn't real! You're not alive!*
just as Cong burst through the brush.
I spin and duck; my left cane slips;
grenades explode around my head. *They're coming!*
Help! I've got no weapon! "Mis-ter? Mis-ter?"
—singsong English, women's faces,
then a man's. I see the bus they rushed from
grind across the can. They help me up.
"O-kay you? Fine? O-kay?" the one who speaks
my language chirps. I nod. *Just take me back*
where I belong!—I don't say that.
I brace myself on the two canes,
repackage who I am within my nervous skin.
"Much thanks"—my grin a scream
I keep inside. I watch their fingers
flutter as they edge away, leave me
to fight in jungles they can't comprehend.

SIGNALS

Scorched hillsides show gnarled black
twistings of burned limbs and roots.
Vultures rise and float on heavy wings
above the "V" where distant valleys merge.
I push the radio atop the crest, peer
through the duck blind openings
we've weaved from vines and camouflage.
Signals from the spotter planes come stronger now.
They want artillery. I watch puffs of smoke
drift towards us, ghosts of this unending war.
"Charlie! Charlie!" pinned down
First Cav interrupt the spotter planes.
I get airborne to come in fast. The hills
along the closest "V" erupt in flames
then smoke so thick it looks like boiling tar.
FOs somewhere along the ridge
bleat "Error! Error!" Across a patch
of burned-out black I catch a surge
like vegetation rising, rolling in a storm.
"Cong!" I start to call—I'm wrong.
In vivid bursting orange of napalm
I see fleeing beings—children, women,
silhouettes against the spreading flames.
Mary-fulluv-grace... some voice nearby
starts moaning. I nod and tell
whoever hears me on the telephone
that's what it costs to win this fucking war.

SUPPLY CLERK

Rain clouds rise and push each other
past the bend of river and the quivering trees
beyond. Framed against them for a moment,
a fat cargo airplane tilts its blunt nose upwards.
Below, a barge rocks to and fro beside a dock
that's still unfinished; power shovels
dip and lift their loads of dripping silt.
I block my thoughts to not hear anything
inside this building—teletypes or typewriters,
phones ringing, voices shouting orders
—rub my fingers on my hemline,
pull a sheaf of papers from a file.
Then put them back. I know the margin notes
and comments, all the *hereons, herewiths,*
confirmations, signatures by heart.
Shiploads of steel, tools and machinery
arrived here...*when?* The dock they're now replacing
broke, collapsed, clogged things so badly
even mail boats couldn't get through.
Yet freighters came and were unloaded?
I sent tracers: lengths and weights and serial numbers;
they all came back *used in construction*
but not a hint of a new building,
road or wharf. *Someone got rich.*
That's what I wrote to my superiors.
Prob'ly stolen by the gooks was their reply.

SECOND LIEUTENANT

A hundred yards beyond the base
the path I follow curves downhill
past the eroded stones of an old mill.
Through leaves that filigree the white dawn light
I sit and eat a doughnut, sip at coffee til it cools,
then climb back to the fence and follow it
to Base Gate 2. A doc stands like a snowman
melting in warm rain, his cigarette a glow
between thick fingertips. "Bad day?" I ask.
"Lost one." He flips the burning butt away.
"A girl, fifteen or so I'd guess. Some hot-rod
fucking dunderhead rammed a big earth mover
with an eight-foot plow straight through her hut.
She fell, got caught beneath the blade.
He heard her scream, backed up, then gunned
the thing and dragged her thirty, forty feet.
She was a mess, but still alive until..."
He shrugs. "Her brother, mother, they're in there."
I want to touch his arm, say something kind;
instead I wipe the grounds out of my cup and go inside.
Two armed MPs have a young Vietnamese
choke-held, coughing, on his knees. "What's going on?"
I ask. "Fuckin' gook tried to attack!"
"Let him go," I tell the guards. "He works on base."
Melanian knuckles close so tight
the bones beneath them glisten through the skin
as he gets up, stumbles towards the rag
of a woman by the door. Her face is torn
by scathing shrieks that set my teeth
on edge—a dentist's drill. Bone-thin arms
around his neck, she calls to someone—something—
far beyond what I can hear or understand.
"Write the motherfucker up..." one MP gruffs.

I turn and glare. "Write the jerk who killed her up,"
my voice so cold it hurts my throat.
The MP twitches, makes a fist, exclaims,
"He's just a gook!" "No, he's a..."
human being just like us you foul-mouthed jerk!
I start to snap but blazing eyes—the boy's—
impale me with their stare. I know that, burned
within my mind, he's there to stay. I bow my head.

AMBUSH

A culvert oozing thick black mud
spreads past twists of rusted steel
and bottoms out in clumped swamp grass.
A motorbike with a baggage rack made
of old orange crates putts past.
Two farmers cross the road and disappear.
"Hey! There's Jacot!" the corporal yells.
I turn. The big Marine is trotting up the road.
The way his pack and canteens bounce across his stride
reminds me of a water boy at a football game.
I laugh—a grunted sort of cough
the others imitate until we see his face.
"Wha-wha-what's wrong?" we stammer
all at once. His lips twist back,
expose the tips of his white teeth;
glasses fogged with steam and sweat
reptile his eyes. "Tha-that fucking place..."
he starts, then shakes his head and starts again.
"Ri-right there, they...they ambushed
a platoon." "Who...what...?" the others interrupt.
I grab his arm. "Tell us..."
He pulls his glasses off his face
and looks at me. "Same fu-fucking
place—the place we stopped,
we—we fucking sat there, ate,
we talked...you—you fucking bowed
—and so did they..." His eyes go off
on a wild flight. "They...what?" I shake
his shoulder hard and he shouts back,
"Cong! Fucking Cong! They fucking killed
at least ten men!" He grabs his weapon,
starts to run, then every muscle
in his body snaps. *And why not us?*

I think I hear—from him, from all the other men.
From inside me as I think back, "We came as friends,
we showed respect..." but it's too late.
Respect is gone. Now we'll retaliate.

NIGHT PATROL

Above the silent jungle-shrouded hill
a scythe-like tiny sliver disappears
into the clouds. I feel a quiver
ricochet through nerves
trained just to see, not feel. The moon
will do that when you're flying
—get inside your skin. Its crescent
glimmers on the water
as we tilt lower, wing tips
scraping tree tops, hear a burst
of fire, veer away unhit. In the darkness
creeks and rivers glisten—veins of luminescent jade
spreading through the dark. Once we blew apart
three tiers of thickest jungle
—Gatling guns and cannons, rockets, CBUs—
out crumbled an old temple no one knew
was there. Past the hill, metallic glimmers
hint at trucks or tanks or cannons.
I yank the stick, pull upwards, veer around
to blast the jungle, empty everything we've got.
Then climb, the back-seat guy behind me
shouting that our rudder's ripped
from small arms' fire. I nod,
follow creeks and shadows,
wobbling, praying, watching Delta rivers
widen, lead us back to base.

WHY?

The cheers. Just listen to the cheers!
The rahs go back and forth from deck
to deck. "The fuckin' gooks!" some guy
beside me in the bomb room spits.
"War's over now...we'll all go home..."
but deep inside the feeling isn't good.
I'm not sure why. It's just that
...if it's over, then—what did it mean?
For months the crew I'm on's been loading bombs
and watching planes take off,
come back, load up and fly again.
Now they won't...be doing that.
Now...now, inside, I'm sort of...like you get
when you're a kid and think you're winning
some big prize and it turns out to be
some hokey cardboard thing.
We went all out. We really did. And...now?
It's over, man. The whole shebang
...like a prom date and, man!
the music's mediocre and you walk away
and she says, "Thanks," and you drive home
and catch the final inning
of a game the Dodgers lose. So what?
You want an ending that explodes.
Not hunched mid-decks with dirty hands,
your thoughts on *why?* and *who am I?*
and all those bombs the warplanes dropped
and who they may have killed.

DAY AFTER CEASE-FIRE

The river bleeds a reddish mud so thick
it curdles past our prow and leaves a wake
of churned up ridges stretching shore to shore.
Monkeys in the jungle screech
and birds with raucous voices answer.
"Spooky, man!" Kaps fiddles with the radio.
I nod. No planes, no guns, just silence
closing in around our engine's softly throbbing pulse.
"What if...?" Talk, the gunner, wets his lips
but doesn't add "...they shoot and we can't
fire back?" I nod to let him know
I'm thinking the same thoughts: It should be over
but we're still out here looking
for some jerk who took a bird out on his own
and got himself shot up. "Okay," Kaps grunts,
"they heard from him again." Fifteen,
sixteen knots away, alone, inland;
because of the cease-fire Airborne's afraid
to take the copters in. "They're going to try
to talk him to a spot where we can get him..."
Kaps lets the sentence lapse. Close to the bank
we glide past growth so thick the wadded green
exudes a throbbing heat. Birds' chatter
sounds like strafing guns. An air-sea rescue plane
dips past; we wave, talk points.
There's open river up ahead. Balls up the wall
we swerve around a jut of land
the NVA had occupied a week or two before
but no one shoots, no one shouts.
Field glasses up, I scan ahead.
We're close now to the pick-up point
—and scared. Each splash, each chirp,
each monkey yell grabs at our guts.

"Oh shit!" Kaps pulls at his cheeks
with ragged fingernails, "They got him, sir,"
trying not to choke. "Who?" "NVA."
"We could..." *go in* I hesitate
but it's too late, HQ has called
the mission off. Kaps shakes his head.
I sigh, then push the throttle up. Behind us,
in the sweltering green, monkeys
taunt us with their hideous screams.

<<<
AN ENEMY TO BLAME
>>>

BABY BOOMER DENTIST

Government: It's like a growth with tentacles
invading everything we do. We chop them off,
the tentacles grow back—or push out
somewhere else. We do it to ourselves:
submerge identity within the greater form
that we call state and nation, city, town
then abdicate what's really ours: control.
To stop the beast we've got to drive a sword
through its devouring heart then start again,
piece by piece, with what we need
and what we want—and what we won't condone.

8:45 p.m. Rustic terrace, good hashish,
    graying educated friends
    laughing up old hippie shtick.

10:15 p.m. Last stories told, familial goodbyes,
    warming cup of ginseng tea,
    moon a fingernail against the glassy night.

10:45 a.m. Drills counterpointing muted music.
    Chipped and crooked, missing, rotten teeth.
    Eight percent *pro bono*—welfare mothers, kids.

The more efficient government becomes,
the more its managers eviscerate
the disparate parts. A vote is currency—
a way to pay for what we want
and what we choose: sidewalks or none,
sewers, gun control, traffic lights.
Eliminate the faceless neuters telling us
what we should do:
                  make each person his own law
to live just as he chooses, setting his own rules.

TELEPHONE INSTALLER

Government's a swamp. Too many people,
not enough to do. They act like cops
who think we're criminals—not working Joes
trying to add a fence, a deck, upgrade our houses
so our kids will have a decent place to live
—slap us with assessments, sewer charges,
tell us how to pave our driveways,
fine us if they find us stringing
this or that extension cord. Then tell us,
"Hey! Your property's gone up in price!
We'll have to tax you more!"

5:30 p.m. Air-conditioned darkness,
    beer and whiskey-saturated wood.
    Coarse inviting laughter,
    familiar faces up and down the bar.

5 a.m. Aspirin. Silver sliver
    of the disappearing moon.
    Wife and daughter sleeping
    in their separate walled-off worlds.

11:45 a.m. Lunch-time quick ones
    in "The Tavern," half-a-sandwich lunch.
    Tip confirms bartender's silence. Back
    on the job, jaws working strong clove gum.

3:45 p.m. One more quick one.
    Cell phone crackling trouble call.
    Fumbling fingers splicing
    old equipment onto new.

My house'd be an eyesore sure
except I took it on myself to fix it up
real good. Hey! Give a man a chance,

I say. Taxes stifle everything
ambition generates. We work; we build;
we pay the salaries of the half-assed idiots
who sit around all day doodling on computer pads
between their coffee breaks. We pay
for them and hundreds more who stay
at home and pop out kids. Any business
would go broke run the way this county's run.

ACCOUNT CLERK

Of course I sympathize with their complaints.
I've got two kids, a pregnant wife, a house
I'm trying to build myself. I try to tell them
hey, I understand: Taxes seem too high,
so do grocery prices, car repairs, union dues—
but they just look away, think they're getting screwed
because a "Mexican" works here. They want to talk
to someone else. My supervisor's good:
she listens, sympathizes, shrugs—or sighs—
agrees about inequities, the people
who inflation helped and those inflation hurt
while I try to mollify another diatribe
about bureaucrats' long coffee breaks
and welfare mothers driving Cadillacs
while honest folks like them are forced to work.

7 p.m. "Play ball!" Little Leaguers
    pitch and swing, trip and stumble,
    "Out!" and "Strike!" and "Foul!"
    sweat drenching their blue shirts.

12:30 a.m. Awake to screeching brakes
    —kids hot-rodding down the street—
    wife rinsing the last dishes,
    the rented movie's rewind clicking off.

1:15 p.m. Smock over office clothes,
    paint-splotched blueprints on the floor;
    quick bites on deli taco lunch.

5:45 p.m. McDonald's: "What the hell,
    it's quick!" Son pushing little sister
    on the goofy lion swing.

6:30 p.m. Two hours more of daylight:
    shelves, then sills, then molding.
    Radio on the floor behind him:
    Giants' play-by-play.

I'm just like anybody else: I want a place
my kids can grow up strong and happy,
get good jobs, play ball, have fun.
When things run right there's room
for everyone and no one pays too much.
When things run right. The problem is
some people have too much and some
don't have enough to keep from going nuts.

TEENAGERS

A drag! Hey man, that's school! What do jerks
called teachers know? The way you wear
a Raiders' jacket means your gang
is in control? Low English and stroke gentle to pull
the cue ball back just so? Which condoms
feel the best and where to keep
them in your purse?

I know a guy
who details cars—he's really good. Know what
he earns? More than any college grad
can get!

Half the school's on welfare anyway,
the other half's out selling drugs.

Or working
five four-hour shifts a week at Taco Bell.

A waste of time. C'mon! There's nothing
I can learn by reading Emerson
or Poe.

More use to me are racing cams.
Turquoise earrings.

Sinsemilla stems.

Who gives a shit

what cosine means?

Or when the Continental Congress met?

7:30 p.m. Lakeside hangout. Cokes
    and French fries. Bets on who
    can walk the guard rail
    without falling, getting wet.

2:15 a.m. Ringing cell phone.
    "Oh shit! We'll be right there!"
    Hospital a blur of moans and curses.
    Friends' faces like flayed meat.

40

4:15 a.m. TV a muted flickering
   —old movie on the screen.
   Packs of crackers, pre-cut cheese.
   Mumbled cursings, "Glad
   it wasn't you or me."

Noon. Crowded drive-in: Heavy metal throbbing
   against cranked up Punk. Catnaps
   in the back seat, redoing redone
   makeup in the cramped and dirty john.

I need to know how insects breathe?
Write about good government while friends
strung up to tubes and wires fight for life?
                     Accidents
and child abuse and gang bangs.
                  Half the freshmen girls
I palled around with now are mothers.

Guys get beat up just for hanging out
on the wrong corner.
                Hall permission slips
so I can go off campus during lunch!

Cops on our case for being out past curfew!

Teachers? Parents? Shadows in a world
that never touches how we really feel.
To them we're 4-H Clubs, the Junior Prom,
Please Wait for Sex, Say No to Drugs.
They close their ears when we talk sweat
and sickness coming down from crank,
date rape and clinics that give abortions,
who has AIDS and who they screwed.
Suicide—why not? Is life so goddamned good?

JUNIOR HIGH MUSIC TEACHER

We teachers are a spoiled bunch.
Most of us own houses, boats,
a time-share here and there
or motor home. We rode inflation
like surfers on big swells and, *crash!*
here we are buoyed in opulence
—but nearly broke. We bitch about how much
it costs to send our kids to college,
fantasize retirement in far-away resorts
and try to drive a few important facts
into the craniums of kids who'll never have
the chance to surf those swells the way we did.
It's sad: The only ones among them
who'll attain what we've saved and bought
are those who get it by inheritance,
not by ambition and hard work.

5:15 p.m. Sunlight on the kitchen's tile;
        fingers chopping walnuts; touch
        of brandy in the cheese ball;
        CD piano jazz.

8 p.m. Sherbet, punch and crackers;
        seven friends together; rented movies
        on the centerpiece TV.

11 p.m. Fingers roaming yellowed keys:
        memories of dance bands,
        concert hall performance dreams.

3:30 a.m. Warm milk cure for sleeplessness.
        Wars and floods and accidents,
        the night news on TV.

10 a.m. "One-and-two-and-altogether-now..."
  Hands cadencing the ragged beat,
  inward grimace, outward smile
  as clarinets and trombones squeak.

I don't care what parents say,
it's different now. Try to bust every kid
you think is using drugs and we'd wind up
without a band, without an honor roll,
without athletic teams. Facebook
is more their home than this small town;
music isn't saxophones, it's MTV.
Some day I'd like to lock this band
in a closed room with Eagles tapes,
or Fogerty. Just let them pick and plunk
and toot and scream until they'd learned
all that they could, then kick them out
to play. Why not? These kids
are hip to Twitter, guns, what
the lyrics to rap music really mean.

ENGLISH PROFESSOR

Wait a minute! This is nuts! Creationism
in a high school class? Public education shouldn't
cavil to the doctrines of the right-wing few
—a school board should be lauding
the best teachers, bring in prominent guest speakers,
form alliances with business, government.
Education isn't mimicry and winning football games;
it's using thought and language, mathematics,
hands and eyes and conversation to solve problems.
Kids are curious, virile creatures.
Give them meat and muscle, make them work
—alone, in groups. Let them bruise their fingers
breaking things, then fix their damned mistakes.

4:45 p.m. Basement-office flicking
    computer-screen reflections.
    Twice rewritten footnotes
    window-ed onto pages; wife and son's
    footsteps tromping overhead.

2:15 a.m. Hurt little cries escaping
    from wife's troubled dreams.
    Hand on her shoulder in the darkness
    —memories of fervent mergings,
    rejected Fulbrights, tenure schemes.

3:15 p.m. Politics and pastry
    on associate's new deck.
    Laundry lists of long-lost
    friendships, growing kids.

You can't pour thoughts like chemicals,
measure, mix and demonstrate the product
you've produced. You want smart students,

let them wrestle with the real world
like our fathers had to do. Morality is doing!
Not cowering in corners hoping no one
knows you've bought a condom, puked
on vodka, coughed a joint. Get off their backs
and do your jobs by giving them computers,
movies, chainsaws, smithsonite. And classrooms
filled with angry, joyous, honestly outrageous books!

FOOTBALL COACH

Fake a block and trap the tackle
Just move him out, don't knock him down!
More than a game, football's a way of living
marked with clear, distinct dimensions:
fifteen minutes to a quarter, ten-yard markers,
chalk lines defining out of bounds.
A way of channeling emotion into power
one can use—the thing some parents never learn,
nor people who shout *Waste of money!*
Special treatment for a few!
Learning is a process that begins
like calisthenics—warming up the mind—
rules and how to change a play at the last second,
take advantage of blown coverage,
repetitious weeks of practice bursting
into one game-winning block, reception or return.

10:30 p.m. Bed a boat that takes him
  to familiar shores. Her arms
  entwine with others he has loved.

7:15 a.m. Pull-and-grunt in unison
  with sweating bodies;
  thirty minutes on the heavy weights,
  forty on the bike.

6 p.m. "Run it again!" Patterns they can break
  at the right moment: leap past reason
  into thrills igniting their whole being,
  make them feel like grown-up men.

No one works harder than these kids
or us, who coach on our own time.
Even those among their classmates
who'll go on to property and wealth

won't forget these players' names
or what they did out on the field.
When they become old men on canes
or strapped in convalescent beds,
they'll still hear high school trumpets blare,
feel blood surge as crashing pads
fill their universe with victory cheers.

COUNTY ASSESSOR

Some say government's "too big." Of course it is,
but once it wasn't big enough. No schools
of any kind, roads were rutted tracks,
no bridge across the river. Men saw and understood
these things, decided each should give a portion
for communal good. To make determinations fair
there had to be both laws and rules
and someone who could measure and compute
the value of each mapped-out farm and lot.
By vote they chose that man, and he compressed
their wants and needs into percentages to pay
according to their worth. "Too big?"
Those who pay don't understand
how much they get for what they spend:
safe drinking water, well-paved highways,
jails and cops and football fields.
Animal control. And me, of course.

6 p.m. Sunlight sparkling on crystal
    glasses holding their pre-dinner
    wine. Laughter a restless scurry
    through his wife's impatient eyes.

8:15 p.m. Casual expensive clothes
    —subtle signs of ownership,
    small-town success. Guests' gossip
    shredding theory over decaf coffee drinks.

9 a.m. Stapled papers growing mountains
    on office cabinets. Lawyers
    fencing their insistence
    on the way the process works.

That industry writes off its wealth
and bare subsistence workers can't deduct
the trailer where their children sleep
is politics—not government. You can't condemn
arithmetic for giving the right answer
or a car for taking you somewhere
you didn't want to go. Where there
were hearty pioneers who chose
and paid to build our schools and roads,
airports and water lines, we now
have selfish children finding fault
—but never with themselves. Damned sure
they want what taxes buy as long
as someone else will foot the bill.

REGISTERED NURSE

I've worked in hospitals enough to understand
why rules are made and know that clerks,
accountants, health inspectors, cops
work hard and want the best. I also see
the immigrants with snot-nosed babies
taking up our doctors' time. Welfare mothers
out to calm their weeks of popping crank.
Pregnant dropouts sucking cans of coke,
the bruises from their boyfriends' beatings
darkening their eyes. That I pay taxes to pave
roads, fund nursing homes and AIDS research
I think is great. Not building bombers,
covering up junk bond scams or giving criminals
long trials that wind up causing riots.
I pay the penalty with earnings I could use
to buy new clothes, car tires, stove.
Those who make our laws need boundaries.
Listen to our "no" to what is wrong
and "yes" to what is right.

4:30 p.m. Day-off reading in the bedroom,
    planned-for only child at hiking camp,
    husband still at work.

9:30 p.m. Bedtime story filled with dreams of princes,
    castles, closets jammed with clothes.

2:45 a.m. Sisters bending down
    to shout *useless little brat!*
    Mirrored reflection of her face
    shattering the dream:
    Don't they envy me right now!

7 a.m. After-operation patient
    trying to talk about grown children:
    hand on his, aloof but nodding
    to the rhythm of the frightened words.

Patients close their ears when doctors talk.
"Will I get well?" and "If so, when?"
That's all they want until they get the bill,
then they complain, "Too many tests!"
Berate the doctors, squeal that Medicare's
no good. They do the same with government—
close ears and eyes until a face
or document intrudes: traffic cop, tax auditor,
jury summons, hurricane repayment grant.
One mistake and "Fix it! Fix it! Fix it!"
they all shout. Then turn their backs,
mourn millionaire dead rock stars
while widows without welfare eat
canned cat food in Tenderloin roach flats.

DISABILITY PENSIONER

We bought our "little farm" to have some elbow room.
I worked part-time; my husband left high-tech
to take a teaching job. We gave our daughter
and our son books and laptops, CDs, city trips;
sent them off to college. Insurance covered
all my husband's bills when he got sick
and paid for mine after my accident.
I could live on what I have if I could sell part
of the ten acres but it's not, they say,
"zoned" that way. I have to sell it all
or stay in this huge house and let
the fruit trees bramble into unpicked declarations
of a crippled widow's fight with rules
that serve, amorphously, some "greater good."

8 p.m. Lake view through clubhouse windows:
        attentive waiters, long-time friends,
        lawyers explaining legal problems,
        compliments on newest dress.

11:30 p.m. Electric fans modulating
        medicated darkness; tomcat kneading
        new position on a corner of the bed.

1 p.m. Orchard alive with children
        running back and forth with limbs
        their whistling gardener father's pruned.

We've built society with rules instead of kindness.
Partitioned people into little boxes
we call laws and truth. Why not let every house,
like every student, be itself—grow from within.
Let those who can't acquire mathematics
put together poems, repair cars

52

—do what they most want to do—
and let houses, homes and orchards
shrink into a size that fits their owners
when they're old and barren, then grow
with vigorous new buyers into something
eloquent and grand—condominiums
if need be, TV towers, hospitals. Or nurseries
where orchids, roses, pretty bougainvillea bloom.

WELFARE APPLICANT

Welfare told me, "Get a job." I did.
But Joe, my older boy, got in fights in school.
I pulled him out. I meant to find another school
but working nights, driving trucks
—Hell! I had to sleep sometime! Then he got busted
—just a little bit of pot. I beat his butt so hard
he couldn't sit down. Some days I'd get home
late and he'd be gone—I don't know where.
I tried to hook up with this woman that I met
but Davey—he's the younger—poured syrup
in her underpants and used her earrings
to make fishing hooks. I'd send them
to their mother but she's up north somewhere,
in Oregon, living with a guy who's high on drugs.
The Man says he'll put them in a foster home
if I don't watch them better than I've done.
So I come to the county for some help.
Ain't that what welfare's for?

8:45 p.m. Headlights flicker off the strip mall's neon.
   Coasting in to preserve gas.
   Iranian clerk who can't speak English.
   Two sixers and a pack of cigarettes.

3 a.m. Crash and clatter, *where's the light?*
   Girlfriend wiggling into sweater;
   grumpy coughed goodbyes.

10 a.m. Last bite of sugar-loaded cereal;
   kitchen table lined with carburetor parts.
   Rush Limbaugh turned up loud.

1 p.m. "Eggs Special": local diner hangout
   of mechanics, pensioners. Extra coffee
   without asking: truck and motorcycle talk.

It's not my fault. My dad was nuts.
He ran off from my mom and didn't come back.
She raised me good, and I'd've been okay
except my ex, she ruined me. She didn't want
to be a wife—or mother to the boys.
She wanted out: That's what she said.
She didn't cook, she didn't clean, she didn't supervise
the kids; she just complained about the way
we lived, spent all my money going back to school
then took the credit cards and split. Me and the boys
would be okay given a new start. No debts.
Clean slate at school. Someone at home
to cook for us. A decent car that runs.

SMALL BUSINESS OWNER

Taxes take an awful bite. So does alimony,
child support. Health insurance has gone
out of sight. A guy I hire now and then
pays more to rent a cramped apartment
for his wife and kids than I can pay him
in a month. How the hell do they get by?
Extra jobs, gifts from their folks,
maxed-out credit cards, I guess. They can't afford
long distance calls or central air, cable TV
—things that make our day-to-day existence
bearable. Sure, guys like him curse government.
Their intuitions tell them something's wrong.
People used to loudly boast *American!*
and mean *I'm proud of what my country is!*
What it has and does. Like give us airports.
Freeways. Hire firemen and soldiers,
meat inspectors, cops. Protect, provide,
demand that we participate, identify
with our home town, this state or that,
the West or North or East or South,
and brag *I'm part of where my money went.*
Because of it my country is the best!

9:15 p.m. Flashes through the quonset's windows:
　　　small planes' landing lights.
　　　Aircraft parts along the counter:
　　　not unusual, working half the night.

12:45 a.m. Laughter, crowded hangout,
　　　smoke jumpers, tanker pilots
　　　and their girlfriends, wives.
　　　Old stories absorbing brash new details:
　　　danger; fun-filled forest fire fights.

9 a.m. Scrubbed and shaved and right
    on time for Jeff and Karen,
    their mother tense and curt
    and distant. Admonition:
    Have them back at five!

1:30 p.m. How to explain the other woman?
    Cramped apartment? Brand new car?
    Hey! Come on! I'll buy you something nice!

Unhappy people have to have an enemy to blame;
that's why they curse the government.
The person who feels cheated sees only bad,
not the good that cops and crop inspectors,
health officials, science teachers do.
No doubt we have too many rules
but so do business, industry. I know:
I have to deal with company technicians every day.
They can't pick up a wrench unless they call
their manager, and all he'll talk about is "bottom line"
as though it's a solid stripe somewhere. Business
covers its mistakes by adding to the price of goods
and no one seems to care. But government must do
with less because its users pay according
to their wages and the property they own.
Just like people pulling at the pins
of marriage, taxpayers strain against demands
that once seemed good. So they lash out.
Or whine because this partnership
—man with his fellow man—forces them to be
more than they want to be: parts of a whole.
Their brothers' keeper. Logical and kind.

<<<
BELIEVING IN HIS DREAMS
>>>

WRITER

In that strange in-between, not sleeping
nor yet awake, he reaches towards shelves
lined with books, paintings on the wall,

framed awards and photographs,
then feels them lurch and crumble
as he gropes at shards, shadows,

the not-quite-light of morning colorless,
opaque as squinting reaffirms the commonness
of condo walls, a flower pot, jacket

like a tattered skin hung upon a hook.
His life. Not what he wished but who he is,
still capable of thought. Of work. Of dreams.

MORNING

Grays colliding then dispersing, slow waltz
of dim incipient light. Quietly
he watches, coquettish smiles all that remain

of pleasant dreams, tweaked muscle aching,
sounds of traffic; the cat, awake, hopping
to his lap. Alone but not alone:

daughters' laughter, curtain calls,
teargas clouding fleeing shapes that jerkily
concede their screams to baseball games

then wrinkle into where he is: decrepit couch,
shelves of books, half-filled coffee cup.
He smiles, retrieves the coquette's wink,

daughters' squeals, police attacks, packs them
back where they belong and, stretching, tells
the cat, "It's time." The work day has begun.

REDOING AN OLD HUMOR PIECE

Let's see now… coffee cup, deck of cards
to shuffle while he ponders, notebook
(*no the other one!*), dust the monitor

and *…where in hell…? oh yeah, filed under…*
skim-reads, stops, goes back to what he wrote
and where he wrote it years before,

his life less real than many he has read about
in trashy books or long-lost magazines.
Shrugs aside intentions to expand, update;

corrects a verb and, squinting, sees himself
as he was then, a younger man intent
on writing things as he writes now but, unlike
now, with eagerness. Believing in his dreams.

WORDS

Always words—names and quotes
and paragraphs, assignment notes (*two thou max,*
five Cs on pub) the same as forty years before

(baseball flacks, indigenous ghosts,
welfare fraud) money disappearing
as the checks came in (travel costs,

long distance calls, kids needing this or that)
never thought I'd live this long… but here
he is, two-bedroom flat, workmen hammering

a wall next door, his fingers slapping
keyboard nubs…*should have time to finish this…*
then clinic visit, taco stand and back to work

—just like forty years before: names and quotes,
assignment notes, the money always short.

LANGUAGE

Sidetracked by baseball lineups, scores,
the black cat slapping at his toes, he blinks
and looks around: the walls, the floor,

the ceiling joists begin to talk in some strange way,
squeaks and murmurs, whispers, groans. He tries
to listen, understand. Trees outside the window

move, the metal gate makes clicking sounds
and something he can't see begins to laugh.
Shapes flick past, phantoms in the changing light;

the cat leaps up and runs to hide as shadows
clog the space around him, voices surge,
floorboards give way beneath his feet,

and with them he spins into space where sight
becomes a limitation. *So many living,
sentient things!* And he with them for just

that moment, then mere form and structure:
old beams and plaster creaking in the wind.

INTERRUPTION

As though a drowning swimmer
caught by windswept swells, the face
on the computer screen dissolves.

For a moment, frowning, he peers
at the opaqueness, caught in a recurrent
dream: about to step into a brightly lit

and festive place, the scene turns gray,
but he keeps walking towards he knows
not what. *Write another critical account...*

revise old poetry... Despite two marriages,
five healthy and ambitious kids, shelves
of books and monographs—some that he's written,

others gifted, borrowed, bought—
he's where he's been for sixty years,
trying to penetrate that fog, put into words

dissolving shapes that lead the way
to something precious, something that he's lost.

A SIMPLE MEAL

Lentils, rice; clay bowl crafted
on a potter's wheel; he reads while eating
(handicapped by broken teeth),

his one companion a black cat
perched table-side, his memories
like clouds dwindling into scraps

of gray above the building tops.
Content? He doesn't think about it much
nor venture into fantasies

like he once did when he was young.
Enough to eat, books to read,
life like fishing in the river:

maybe catch a perch, a carp
or nothing more than warming sun,
phantom clouds, the sudden flight of doves.

FRIENDS APPEAR

and join him at the table: children, father,
mother, workmates, uninvited but a presence,
constant, like a chorus, dictums, thank yous,
praise and longings on their tongues.
                                    He speaks
to them, grapes and cheese and grapefruit passing
plate to spoon to mouth, each word evoking
memories that answer what he says,
then change as though alive, part of a fluid
world of constant alterations like his life
—or lives—each moment just a drop of rain,
each word, each grape, each smile.

BEST FRIEND

A blue-eyed precocious little guy finds
a place within my space to play. I nod,
amused—he looks like who I used to be—
then realize the room has changed

and I'm behind the corner of a sofa
in the house where I grew up
recording hits and outs—my baseball game—
content, alone, far from the what-to-wear

and who-said-what among my parents' friends.
But not alone. There's someone there. I talk
to him; we play, compete. But he's not real!
Who told me that? He's real to me! My pal!

My friend! He laughs and I begin to shout
at tigers thrashing through dawn redwoods,
Stukas diving, Shiva waving many arms.
Bob! I hear someone calling, stop, return
to writing, flat and cheated by his leaving.

Yes! I respond to wife and son, neighbors,
errands, dishes, fix the roof: these and other
deviations from adventure, laughter, dangers
as I jive again in his and my real world.

WHEN HE WAS JUST A TYKE

Sunday morning was a favorite time.
Sprawled on the rug, the comics mapping worlds
incredible and vast: Prince Valiant
in his armored vest, Orphan Annie
with her Sandy dog, jut-jawed Dick Tracy's
knowing squint.

        Like dancers curtained
behind gauze, they whisk along the pockmarked
wall and for a moment he is child
enmeshed in futures wondrous,
                  vast,
not this (though pleasant) growing old
—old without futures, only pasts.

            He wipes
his face, wanting both to be back there
and to apologize—for what he isn't sure.
Lost dreams perhaps. Or lost belief.
The comics meant so much.

AGNOSTIC

Rain so soft he barely hears its whispers
on the windowsill. Clouds like shadows
in a dream of something unperceived

that he should recognize. In front of him,
baseball scores from cities far away,
the cat curled on a box of books asleep,

coffee warm against his fingertips,
the past obscured, intangible,
the future a mere glimmering, sun

through undulating fog. A dog
yips once, a truck somewhere accelerates,
he turns, expecting... *what?* He doesn't know,

a sign perhaps, an omen, promise, threat,
the passing breath of something like a god.

SANTA CRUZ AMILPAS, OAXACA

At the curb young mothers laughing, groping
for their children's hands, bus headlights
in the after-rain a swashed distortion

as it bumbles over bumps. Children first,
the mothers climb aboard; one squeals
as the bus lurches, stops then, honking, toads

into the traffic flow. An old man hunched
beside a rusting dumpster lifts one hand
and, with the other, counts his fingers,

folds them, then counts again. A taxi honks,
dogs race across the street, the owner
of the beer and soda store leans

against an iron grate, cell phone pegged
against one ear. *Wars somewhere? Narcotics
busts?* Neither sparrows in the junipers

nor the old woman in a wheelchair knows.
Just night will come, moon hazed by clouds,
the scent of new-mown hay.

MONTHLY CHECKUP

As he waits he senses dimming lights,
nurses floating wordlessly along the aisle,
walls dissolving into liquid streams

that wash against his shoes and wrap
around his ankles, knees. He falls trying
to swim, awash in yellow, undulating green,

calls for help clogging in his throat...
then hears a name—his name. *Tevoyapesar...*
Te...voy...a...pesar... "I'll weigh you now..."

the room a barren lack of color,
receptionist rising from blurs and splotches
on her computer screen. *Pues sí...*

he answers, stepping on the scales
and sinking into swirling caves
of monstrous fish and ravaged boats...

Sesentaydos... His weight? Her name?
He doesn't know, just hopes his tests are clean.

OBITUARY: FREEDOM FIGHTER

For Bertha Muñoz

Gray the walls, the parquet floor, snapshots
beneath table's glass, gray their faces
as they talk, the three of them, gray

the memories of she who died, old like them,
luchadora, gray the pauses among names,
places, years, the *she was there...* the *I almost...*

their voices but a quiet sea lapping
weathered rocks. Chants and shouts and upraised
fists a flickering gray, remembered, shared

—but far away. One leans against her cane,
another shoulders straight, hands on knees,
the third twicking his short beard,

the times that she... and *threatened rape...*
and nods and words and gray the loss their voices
knead *...of her, of us. Of who we tried to be.*

SURVIVOR

Beer lifted to the setting sun's
diminished light *Alone is bad?* he asks,
cap doffed to show a forehead

marked with scars as though wives, lovers,
others he'd deceived had broken plates
and dishes there. Of course they laugh,

these friends of his, mechanics, painters,
teachers gathered for a holiday's dispense
from work, each envious in his own way

but with a home to go to, not empty rooms,
CDs, a hungry cat. Nor does he tell them
dreams and memories of winks, acceptances,

awakenings in other beds. Just *This is me,*
I'm what you see, no yearning, no regrets
for losing that strange love that's known as *us.*

DIFFERENT

Summer rain a timpani on rusted
roofs of shanties propped against the ridge.
A dog begins to bark, and then another;

smoke from charcoal braziers brings the smell
of hot tortillas, sizzling grease. Inside a hut
someone begins to sing and children laugh;

two teenagers rush past, shared coat
above their heads. Suddenly they swerve
into each other's grasp and kiss, then plunge

on through the rain. Watching them
he smiles, remembering lives past,
then shoulders hunched detours

along a crumbling wall and down the slope
to where he lives, a house of solid brick.

FAN

Rookie errors, relief ace shelled... he shrugs,
day-in, day-out the baseball scores, how many years?
he asks himself, the screen in front of him

now blank. Ferris Fain, Dom DiMag...
names come back then vanish like the names
of high school friends. So far away

and yet as real as people he talked to yesterday
...more real perhaps. Mind and memories
a convolution, never a straight path,

the future never what it's planned to be,
a swirl of atoms bumping, veering whos
and whats and wheres...

                    He laughs and looks around:

the room like him, worn but sturdy, stacks
of books and papers, empty coffee cup,
and twists his fingers as if to throw a slider

past the batter waiting at the plate.

PHILOSOPHER

Life merely an experiment... he tells
himself, spooning soup he made
without a recipe *...a cell spun off*

from other cells devising from environment
a sense of isolated self
that imitates... he scowls, diverted

by a crow hopping past the window
...imitates what other cells devise
to keep from bumping, getting bruised,

forming pods around themselves...
blinks away remembrances of his ex-wife
...fearing to invent themselves

as something separate... reaches
for his coffee cup, spits out a bone
...but like a snowflake caught amid a storm

of melting flakes... and laughs, remembering
his boyhood home, his wooden sword,
the unicorn that only he could see.

GOURMET AT SEVENTY-NINE

Leftovers... but by design. How else can one
who lives alone have home-cooked beans,
grilled chicken, soup? That or crap dumped out

of cans, tasteless noodles, burrito grease.
I like to cook... he tells himself (there being
no one else to tell) clamoring kids,

heaped plates of pasta, applauding guests
ghosting through the vacant room.
One bean meal more then salad, fruit...

Diverted by old notebook notes, memories
of baseball games, he props his feet on tabletop,
invites himself to share a rich dessert.

A GOOD BOOK

Words disappear into vast linkages
of concepts, thoughts, as reading he too vanishes
from where he sits, all things around him

a mirage, a non-existence, temporal,
incapable of blossoming
beyond the jot in time that he transcends.

Then coming back, perched on the couch,
he senses that he went somewhere
outside of self, and now, returned,

rummages among the husks, words
merely words until they merge
into that other: meanings timeless. Vast.

ALONE IN MEXICO

Dishes washed and put away, coffee
in the cup beside him tepid, almost cold,
he flicks through printed sheets of figures

thinking about baseball games, homework
when his son was young, the owner of a pizza
place who shouted anti-Reagan slurs,

and tells the cat how strange life is, how one
winds up far from where he thought he'd be;
then, looking back, remembers one night

crouching under thatch, beer in hand,
and picturing a little place in Mexico,
time to write, banana trees, someone

playing a guitar. *Destiny...*
he tells himself, then shakes his head: more
like a pitch that someone fields—or doesn't:

The ball's in play but no one knows the score.

A MILLION DANCING LIGHTS

Through a crowded dream he sees someone
he knows. Calls out but has no voice,
tries to wave but cannot lift his hand. The figure

seems to pause, look back and then descend
some sort of stairs between medieval walls
that smell of dampness and decay. He hesitates,

then follows, the figure almost out of sight.
Stones crumble into powder with each step.
Wait! he shouts; again the figure pauses,

turns—a shimmering face, a million tiny
dancing lights—then takes a final step
and disappears. The staircase ends,

the walls dissolve, and he emerges
from the dream as empty as a locust husk
whisked by a vagrant wind.

THE OTHER

Three stories down a solitary figure
pauses and looks up as he, alone,
looks down and for a moment is the one

beneath the streetlight looking up. Seeing
only silhouette and frowning wonders
who is it up there? Responds *it's me*

and who are you? as from the window looking
down remembers highrise city streets
and endless windows' lighted squares

and he alone looking up as he, alone,
peers down at him who shrugs and turns
then stops and, looking back, conveys

you should remember: I am you
and disappears as, looking up,
he sees the lights go out.

ACKNOWLEDGMENTS

I am grateful to the following journals where some of these poems first appeared:

Abbey: "A Million Dancing Lights," "Language"
Borderlands: Section 1 of "Good Reports"
California Quarterly: "Monthly Checkup," "Purple Heart"
Cape Rock: "A Good Book"
Exit 13: "Best Friend"
Illya's Honey: "Santa Cruz Amilpas, Oaxaca," "A Simple Meal"
Red Ochre Lit: "Obituary: Freedom Fighter"
Rockford Review: "Different," "Messenger"
Third Wednesday: "Survivor"
Thorny Locust: "Friends Appear"

Cover artwork, "Spirit People," by Dominic Alves; cover and interior book design by Diane Kistner; Highlander text and AnuDaw titling

ABOUT FUTURECYCLE PRESS

FutureCycle Press is dedicated to publishing lasting English-language poetry books, chapbooks, and anthologies in both print-on-demand and ebook formats. Founded in 2007 by long-time independent editor/publishers and partners Diane Kistner and Robert S. King, the press incorporated as a nonprofit in 2012. A number of our editors are distinguished poets and writers in their own right, and we have been actively involved in the small press movement going back to the early seventies.

The FutureCycle Poetry Book Prize and honorarium is awarded annually for the best full-length volume of poetry we publish in a calendar year. Introduced in 2013, our Good Works projects are anthologies devoted to issues of universal significance, with all proceeds donated to a related worthy cause. Our Selected Poems series highlights contemporary poets with a substantial body of work to their credit; with this series we strive to resurrect work that has had limited distribution and is now out of print.

We are dedicated to giving all of the authors we publish the care their work deserves, making our catalog of titles the most diverse and distinguished it can be, and paying forward any earnings to fund more great books.

We've learned a few things about independent publishing over the years. We've also evolved a unique, resilient publishing model that allows us to focus mainly on vetting and preserving for posterity the most books of exceptional quality without becoming overwhelmed with bookkeeping and mailing, fundraising activities, or taxing editorial and production "bubbles." To find out more about what we are doing, come see us at www.futurecycle.org.

THE FUTURECYCLE POETRY BOOK PRIZE

All full-length volumes of poetry published by FutureCycle Press in a given calendar year are considered for the annual FutureCycle Poetry Book Prize. This allows us to consider each submission on its own merits, outside of the context of a contest. Too, the judges see the finished book, which will have benefitted from the beautiful book design and strong editorial gloss we are famous for.

The book ranked the best in judging is announced as the prize-winner in the subsequent year. There is no fixed monetary award; instead, the winning poet receives an honorarium of 20% of the total net royalties from all poetry books and chapbooks the press sold online in the year the winning book was published. The winner is also accorded the honor of being on the panel of judges for the next year's competition; all judges receive copies of all contending books to keep for their personal library.

www.ingramcontent.com/pod-product-compliance
Lightning Source LLC
Chambersburg PA
CBHW070007100426
42741CB00012B/3134